THE DREAM OF A SUMMER NIGHT

Borgo Press Books Edited & Translated by FRANK J. MORLOCK

Anna Karenina: A Play in Five Acts, by Edmond Guiraud, from Leo Tolstoy
Anthony: A Play in Five Acts, by Alexandre Dumas, Père
The Children of Captain Grant: A Play in Five Acts, by Jules Verne and Adolphe d'Ennery
Crime and Punishment: A Play in Three Acts, by Frank J. Morlock, from Fyodor Dostoyevsky
Don Quixote: A Play in Three Acts, by Victorien Sardou, from Miguel de Cervantes
The Dream of a Summer Night: A Fantasy Play in Three Acts, by Paul Meurice
Falstaff: A Play in Four Acts, by William Shakespeare, John Dennis, William Kendrick, and Frank J. Morlock
The Idiot: A Play in Three Acts, by Frank J. Morlock, from Fyodor Dostoyevsky
Jesus of Nazareth: A Play in Three Acts, by Paul Demasy
The Jew of Venice: A Play in Five Acts, by Ferdinand Dugué
Joan of Arc: A Play in Five Acts, by Charles Desnoyer
The Lily of the Valley: A Play in Five Acts, by Théodore Barrière and Arthur de Beauplan, from Honoré de Balzac
Lord Byron in Venice: A Play in Three Acts, by Jacques Ancelot
Louis XIV and the Affair of the Poisons: A Play in Five Acts, by Victorien Sardou
The Man Who Saw the Devil: A Play in Two Acts, by Gaston Leroux
Mathias Sandorf: A Play in Three Acts, by Jules Verne and William Busnach
Michael Strogoff: A Play in Five Acts, by Jules Verne and Adolphe d'Ennery
Les Misérables: A Play in Two Acts, by Victor Hugo, Paul Meurice, and Charles Victor Hugo
The Mysteries of Paris: A Play in Five Acts, by Eugène Sue and Prosper Dinaux
Ninety-Three: A Play in Four Acts, by Victor Hugo and Paul Meurice
Notes from the Underground: A Play in Two Acts, by Frank J. Morlock, from Fyodor Dostoyevsky
Outrageous Women: Lady MacBeth and Other French Plays, edited by Frank J. Morlock
Peau de Chagrin: A Play in Five Acts, by Louis Judicis, from Honoré de Balzac
A Raw Youth: A Play in Five Acts, by Frank J. Morlock, from Fyodor Dostoyevsky
Richard Darlington: A Play in Three Acts, by Alexandre Dumas, Père
The San Felice: A Play in Five Acts, by Maurice Drack, from Alexander Dumas, Père
Saul and David: A Play in Five Acts, by Voltaire
Shylock, the Merchant of Venice: A Play in Three Acts, by Alfred de Vigny
Socrates: A Play in Three Acts, by Voltaire
The Stendhal Hamlet Scenarios and Other Shakespearean Shorts from the French, edited by Frank J. Morlock
A Summer Night's Dream: A Play in Three Acts, by Joseph-Bernard Rosier and Adolphe de Leuwen
Urbain Grandier: A Play in Four Acts, by Alexandre Dumas, Père
The Voyage Through the Impossible: A Play in Three Acts, by Jules Verne and Adolphe d'Ennery
The Whites and the Blues: A Play in Five Acts, by Alexandre Dumas, Père
William Shakespeare: A Play in Six Acts, by Ferdinand Dugué

THE DREAM OF A SUMMER NIGHT

A Fantasy Play in Three Acts

by

Paul Meurice

Translated and Adapted by Frank J. Morlock

THE BORGO PRESS

An Imprint of Wildside Press LLC

MMX

Copyright © 2007, 2010 by Frank J. Morlock

All rights reserved. No part of this book may be reproduced without the expressed written consent of the author. Professionals are warned that this material, being fully protected under the copyright laws of the United States of America, and all other countries of the Berne and Universal Copyright Convention, is subject to a royalty. All rights, including all forms of performance now existing or later invented, but not limited to professional, amateur, recording, motion picture, recitation, public reading, radio, television broadcasting, DVD, and Role Playing Games, and all rights of translation into foreign languages, are expressly reserved. Particular emphasis is placed on the question of readings, and all uses of these plays by educational institutions, permission for which must be secured in advance from the author's publisher, Wildside Press, 9710 Traville Gateway Dr. #234, Rockville, MD 20850 (phone 301-762-1305).

www.wildsidebooks.com

FIRST WILDSIDE EDITION

CONTENTS

Cast of Characters 7

Act I, Scene 1 9

Act I, Scene 2 29

Act I, Scene 3 49

Act II, Scene 4 58

Act II, Scene 5 84

Act III, Scene 6 88

Act III, Scene 7 106

Act III, Scene 8 119

About the Author 123

DEDICATION

TO

MY SWEET GRANDDAUGHTER,

MIRANDA,

WITH LOVE

CAST OF CHARACTERS

OBERON, King of the Fairies

TITANIA, Queen of the Fairies

PUCK, a goblin

FIRST FAIRY

SECOND FAIRY

THESEUS, King of Athens

HIPPOLYTA, Queen of the Amazons

AEGEUS

HERMIA, his daughter

HELENA

LYSANDER

DEMETRIUS

BOTTOM, a shoemaker

LECOING, carpenter

GROIN, Tinker

ETRIGNE, joiner

LAFAMINE, Tailor

FLUTE

MOONBEAM

THE WALL

Fairies, Elves, Goblins, Athenians, Amazons.

ACT I

Scene 1

Scene: in Athens during the Pagan Renaissance.

A room in the palace of Theseus. A cutaway at the right of a throne on a dais. Hippolyta is seated on the throne. Theseus bows before her.

THESEUS:

Beautiful Hippolyta, formidable Amazon, with your arm as powerful as it is white, you have succeeded in making your sex mistress of mine, therefore to maintain the original hierarchies in creation, it was given to me to subdue at the same time both your arm and your heart. Don't complain over your defeat, dear enemy, it is the beginning of your victory. You have conquered your conqueror. He declared war on you only to declare his love, and now he is at your feet, until his prisoner deigns to receive the ransom.

HIPPOLYTA:

Illustrious Duke of Athens, because the luck of arms has made you master, I am happy and proud to be your subject. Come, sit beside me, generous Theseus. To say that I am grateful to my conqueror would be too little. I love him.

THESEUS:

You hear, Athenians! Rejoice! It's peace. And not merely peace, but alliance, and not merely alliance but marriage. Tomorrow, Athenians, your Duke is marrying the Queen of the Amazons. Tomorrow at break of day, I will lead Hippolyta to the palace that I've constructed on the hill, and this happy wedding will be inaugurated.

ALL:

Long live Theseus! Long Live Hippolyta!

THESEUS:

And now let Athens resound with shouts of joy and festive songs. Let the intoxication of my overflowing heart spread over all my people. Let all the amorous couples and fiancés of the town come forward and declare themselves; let them be married at the same time as their prince. My joy is such that it would like the universe to be happy!

AEGEUS: (coming forward)

Great Theseus, our renowned Duke, I am coming like a father to summon the law for one of these marriages.

THESEUS:

Speak, my brave Aegeus.

AEGEUS:

I am coming paternally to denounce my daughter Hermia. Come forward, Demetrius. Milord, this young man has my consent to marry her. He is very rich, he has rich pastures, and fat herds on these pastures. My daughter pleased him, and he pleased me, the father. Come forward, Lysander. This one, my gracious Duke, has surprised and stolen the heart of my child. And with what, I beg you? With bouquets, with candies, with hair, with stupid things, with verse. My conclusion's simple. I'm kicking out the thief, and in the person of my daughter, I am marrying the proprietor.

THESEUS:

What reason have you to give, Lysander?

LYSANDER:

I love Hermia.

DEMETRIUS:

That's not a reason; me, too, I love Hermia.

HERMIA:

Yes, but as for me, Hermia, I do not love Demetrius, I love Lysander.

LYSANDER:

And it wasn't very long ago that Demetrius was in love with another; he was promised to another, he was supposed to marry his cousin, Helena.

THESEUS:

Indeed, I heard that said. I see Helena there, in the crowd. Come forward, Helena.

HELENA:

Milord is calling me?

THESEUS:

Yes. And now, good Helena, speak.

HELENA:

Milord is questioning me, I am really obliged to reply to him, Demetrius, and besides, I am alone. I no longer have my father or my mother, and you are the last relative I have remaining to me. Yes, Milord, I must agree that our fathers, who were brothers, made us fiancées as children. Once upon a time Demetrius wasn't bothered about it. And he said I was his little wife. Now he no longer says that to me. Oh, I accuse no one. I don't accuse Hermia. Hermia doesn't love Demetrius; I love Hermia. I don't even accuse Demetrius. I know quite well that I don't have Hermia's wit. But Hermia doesn't have my heart. Hermia's wit is for all, and my heart is completely for Demetrius.

HIPPOLYTA: (to Theseus)

Poor child! Her gentleness and her pain touch me. Use your authority, my dear Duke. Give Hermia to Lysander and return Demetrius to Helena.

THESEUS:

I would like to do it, my queen, to please you, but above the authority of the prince, there's the law of the city.

AEGEUS:

Wise words! The law, yes. I invoke the fine, virtuous law of Athens, which gives to a father sovereign power over his children.

THESEUS:

That being the case, Hermia, you have no other choice except between Demetrius and the cloister. I see no other exit.

LYSANDER:

Excuse me, there's still this one, noble Duke. It's that I kill Demetrius or that Demetrius kills me.

DEMETRIUS:

Ah! Lysander, you've captured Hermia's heart, and I curse you. But you are offering me an opportunity to take your life, and I thank you for it.

THESEUS: (rising with rage)

What's this mean? When I proclaim peace, behold one who reawakens war.

LYSANDER:

Milord—

THESEUS:

Silence! Tomorrow let Aegeus consent to give Hermia to Lysander and that Demetrious return to Helena. That's what I wish. Hermia will be married to Demetrius or will be vowed to Diana. That's what I command.

(Demetrius and Lysander threaten each other with gestures)

THESEUS:

Follow me, Demetrius; you, too, Aegeus. I have to give you both instructions for the nuptial feast. Come, my Hippolyta.

HIPPOLYTA: (low to Theseus)

My Duke, to be a warrior one is not less a woman, and I admit to you that I am interested in this divided amour.

THESEUS: (low)

Oh! And, me, too. You've already seen. Let's hope that everything falls out in accordance with your wishes, my queen.

(Exit Theseus, Hippolyta, Aegeus, Demetrius, and their suits)

HELENA:

Lucky Hermia! The one you love loves you.

HERMIA:

If I were to say: Lucky Helena, the one you love can marry you.

HELENA:

Yes! Except the one I can marry doesn't love me.

HERMIA:

And me! I can marry only the one I love! Ah, the condition of love in this world is, in truth, very fatal and very cruel. Here love has against it the difference in birth, fortune, rank, or age. There war, illness, death; besides the indifference or the inconstancy of the being loved. Love never goes without sorrow, sighs and tears. All the jealous gods battle, overwhelm love. Why? No doubt because, if it was free, and if it was master love would dominate. What am I saying? Love would replace all the gods.

HELENA:

You speak well, Hermia. That's how you charmed Demetrius.

LYSANDER:

You must act as you speak, Hermia. Our love for each other, so harshly oppressed, requires that you free it.

HERMIA:

Speak. What must I do?

LYSANDER:

Listen! You might listen, too, Helena; because, in serving our love, I am serving yours. Hermia, your father is hostile to our marriage; but your father's sister is favorable to it; she dwells seven leagues from here in a village where the law of Athens has no effect. Near her we could get married without obstacle.

HERMIA:

Well, Lysander, let's go to her. I am confiding myself to you, my gentleman.

LYSANDER:

My cherished Hermia.

HERMIA:

Only, Lysander, how between now and tomorrow, could I?

LYSANDER:

As of this evening, escape from your father's house. At the hour of moonrise find me in the forest of Athens, you know where we met at the last May fest. Hermia, will you do it?

HERMIA:

I will be there.

HELENA: (looking toward the back)

Demetrius!

LYSANDER: (with fury)

Demetrius!

HERMIA:

No outburst, Lysander! I am proving my courage to you. Prove your love to me. You go that way, I go this way. Till tonight.

(they leave excitedly in different directions.)

DEMETRIUS: (entering)

Wasn't that Hermia who moved away?

HELENA:

It's Hermia who's fleeing you, my poor Demetrius.

(reaction by Demetrius) Oh, I'm telling you, not to hurt you, no, rather to pity you. Perhaps, also, you may pity me a bit. If you looked over here you would see an anguish parallel to your own.

DEMETRIUS: (eyes fixed on the way Hermia left.)

Helena.

HELENA:

And yet, I'm still more wretched than you. She that you love doesn't love you. But you are loved by another, loved by me. And as for me, who wanted to be loved by you alone in the world; no one loves me! And I sometimes ask myself if you, the one I love, don't hate me.

DEMETRIUS: (still without turning)

I'd have friendship for you, Helena, if you didn't love me.

HELENA:

You prefer to have it in for me and not for her. It's still not my fault if she doesn't love you. I gave her sufficient example.

DEMETRIUS:

If you hadn't loved me, maybe she would love me.

HELENA:

And you're going to ask me to make her love you? Fortunately, I cannot. But for that I'd be capable of doing it. Yes, so that you'd listen to me less coldly, heavens, merely so that you would look at me at this moment, I'd be capable of…. (Demetrius starts to distance himself) You are leaving me! Oh! Don't leave me yet!

DEMETRIUS:

An order of Theseus.

HELENA:

Admit you are going to try to meet her.

(Demetrius takes another step to leave) Wait! If I still could demonstrate that you are wasting your effort and have nothing to hope for?

DEMETRIUS:

You imagine that would be a way to keep me?

HELENA:

Wait! And if I told you Hermia us going to escape you, escape you forever?

DEMETRIUS:

Hermia escape me! Hermia! No, you are lying! No, that would be too painful.

HELENA:

Ah, you see! You see how one suffers.

DEMETRIUS:

Yes, if I were to lose Hermia, I would die.

HELENA:

You, die! Ah, I prefer to give her to you.

DEMETRIUS:

You would do that! You would have that devotion, Helena? Oh, in that case, my gratitude—

HELENA:

Your gratitude! A return of friendship, perhaps, a new beginning.

DEMETRIUS:

Yes, yes, because I see that you can save me from despair. You know something. Speak, speak!

HELENA:

Oh, no, I mustn't.

DEMETRIUS:

Helena! Speak. My dear Helena!

HELENA:

Your dear Helena! Someone's coming. Listen. Tonight at moonrise be in the forest at the Duke's oak. I will be there. But don't call me "My darling Helena" like that any more. Ah! I will tell you everything.

(They separate)

CURTAIN

ACT I

Scene 2

A courtyard in the lodging of a carpenter.

LECOING:

Is all our troupe here?

ETRIGNE:

I don't see Bottom.

FLUTE:

We cannot begin without Bottom.

LECOING:

No, certainly! Of all of us, he's the one with the most wit! Meanwhile, I remind you of the purpose of our meeting. First, for the wedding of our good Duke Theseus and the beautiful Hippolyta, we tradesmen of Athens have thought of performing some pretty little comedy. I'm directed to compose the play, and we are here to—

(Enter Bottom)

GROIN:

Ah! There's Bottom! Hello, Bottom.

ALL:

Hello, Bottom.

BOTTOM:

Hello, my friends, hello! What have you done, Lecoing? Where are you in it?

LECOING: (deferentially)

We were waiting for you, Bottom.

BOTTOM:

Fine. First of all, Lecoing, tell us the title and subject of your play. Method! Method!

LECOING: (pointing to a notebook)

Here's my play. It's called—

BOTTOM:

Lemme see.

(reading) "The very lamentable comedy and cruel death of Pyramus and Thisbe." Great!

That really ought to be amusing! There's something funny it! Now, Lecoing, take the character list and call your actors. The rest of you get in line. Method!

LECOING:

Answer when I call you. Nicholas Bottom.

BOTTOM:

Present. Now the part destined for me, and continue.

LECOING: (giving him his part)

Nicholas Bottom is inscribed for the role of Pyramus.

BOTTOM:

Perfect. Who is this Pyramus? Is he a lover? Is he a tyrant?

LECOING:

A lover! A lover! And one who kills himself for love, even.

BOTTOM:

Ah! Great! Then I'll have to shed some tears to make 'em cry. That's fine. Go on to the others, Lecoing. I regret slightly that Pyramus is not a tyrant all the same! Oh! I would have been terrible! "To death! To death!"

I would have congealed all spines. But continue, will you, Lecoing.

LECOING:

Francis Flute, bellows mender.

FLUTE: (very young, beardless, feminine voice)

Present.

LECOING:

Francis Flute, you will play Thisbe.

FLUTE:

Who's Thisbe? A knight? A captain?

LECOING:

Er, no, she's the lady Pyramus must love.

FLUTE:

A woman. Oh, I beg you don't make me play a woman; my beard will embarrass me.

LECOING:

Bah! You've only to play it with a mask. And you'll use that little squeaky voice that you like.

BOTTOM:

We can play with a mask?

LECOING:

If you like.

BOTTOM: (coming forward excitedly)

Well, in that case, I demand to play Thisbe, too.

(he slowly takes his part to Flute) You will see, I will play with a monstrous true voice. "Ah, Pyramus my cherished lover! Your Thisbe, your cherished Thisbe!"

LECOING:

But Bottom, you can't play Thisbe and Pyramus, lover and beloved at the same time.

BOTTOM:

You think so? That's a shame! But for the love of God, Lecoing, continue!

(he takes his part back from Flute)

LECOING:

Thomas Groin, tinker.

GROIN:

Here.

LECOING:

Groin, you will be Pyramus' father; as for me, Thisbe's father.

BOTTOM: (momentarily tempted)

The fathers? No, I'd be too old.

LECOING:

Robin Lafamine, tailor.

LAFAMINE:

Present.

LECOING:

Robin Lafamine, you will play Thisbe's mother.

BOTTOM:

Thisbe's mother. (delighted) I'd be ugly.

LECOING:

Etrigne, joiner. You'll have the role of the lion.

BOTTOM:

The role of the lion.

LECOING:

Yes, the role of the lion, who has to terrify Thisbe and tear her cloak from her.

ETRIGNE:

Haven't you written the role for the lion? If it's copied, give it to me 'cause I'm a slow learner.

LECOING:

You will improvise it; it's simply a question of roaring.

BOTTOM:

Ah, I too, want to play the lion. Oh, I would roar so naturally! Listen!

(he roars twice)

ROAARRRR! ROAAARRR! And the Duke and the Duchess will stomp and shout! Bravo! Well roared lion! Well roared Do it again. Encore! ROARRR!

LECOING:

Oh, very nice! But if you roar so uproariously, Bottom, you will frighten the ladies and one mustn't do that because our mothers won't each have a son hanged.

BOTTOM:

That's true, Lecoing, you've got a thought there, that's true. But in that case, don't worry! I will soften my voice in a manner to coo; the roaring of a pigeon. I will roar so's to make you believe that you are listening in Arcadian thickets to a nightingale.

LECOING:

All the same, Bottom, you would do better to play only Pyramus. A very suave man, that Pyramus, get out!

BOTTOM:

Yes, he's indeed my cup of tea, and I'll answer for it. What color beard would become me most in that role?

LECOING:

Whatever you like.

BOTTOM:

Ah, I know, I will put—. The ladies will like it. I will put on an orange colored beard.

LECOING:

Bottom, there are just one or two small difficulties which stop me. The book says that Pyramus and Thisbe are chatting through an opening in the wall. How are we to portray the wall?

FLUTE:

We can never carry a wall on stage. Get yourself out of that, Bottom.

BOTTOM: (after having considered)

Behold! It will be necessary to smear one of us with plaster and whitewash; he will be supposed to be the wall; he'll hold his fingers like so. And Pyramus and Thisbe will whisper through the opening.

LECOING:

Perfect! Perfect! Now, Pyramus and Thisbe in the story meet in moonlight. But how to make the moon fall on the stage?

BOTTOM:

Hey, that's quite simple! Everyone knows there's a man on the moon who carries a bundle of thorns and on the full moon he's seen as if he were there. Some say he's Cain, others that he's the Wandering Jew, but science is uncertain on this point. Well, all we need do to represent him is to have a man with a bundle, and he'll hold a lantern which will be the moonlight.

(General approval)

LECOING:

Oh, admirable, admirable!

GROIN:

But, 'scuse me, if one sees a man with a bundle on the moon, the actor must place himself inside the lantern.

GENERAL PROTESTS:

"Ah, bah!"

LECOING:

Ah, now then, you all have your parts; it will be good to have a rehearsal tonight.

FLUTE:

Where will we meet?

LECOING:

If it's in Athens we will be the objects of curiosity. I propose the forest.

BOTTOM:

Oh, no, not the forest! Not the forest!

LECOING:

Why's that? Is there something terrible in the forest?

ETRIGNE:

Robbers?

LECOING:

Vipers?

FLUTE:

Spiders?

BOTTOM:

Er, no.

LECOING:

Then why reject the forest?

BOTTOM:

Why? My God! It's not so much that it's poisoned by a bunch of flowers and fresh plants which will give us migraines, it's not even because warblers are gathered there, and nightingales who are going to warble all night.

(gathering them around him in terror) Don't you know it's a forest infected with fairies?

FLUTE:

Oh! They say fairies are really pretty.

BOTTOM:

Young man (he pulls him out of the circle): these people are known to be in the shade of morality.

LECOING:

Yes, the forest of Athens, from what is told, is the conjugal domicile of Oberon, King of genies who has his self styled spouse Titania, queen of the fairies, and I am left to say they are perpetually squabbling and they are making almost as fine a household as the Sun and the Moon. When one rise—

BOTTOM:

Deplorable example.

FLUTE: (who comes closer to listen.)

Still—

BOTTOM:

Young man! Honest citizen, imagine yourself seated, unsuspecting, on the grass in this forest, you hear mechanically an acorn in the shadows and suddenly you place your hand on— (with horror) Oh-ah!

FLUTE:

On a little fairy, oh!

BOTTOM:

Young man!

LECOING:

I respect your scruples, virtuous Bottom. But your chastity, my modest friend, is above all temptation.

BOTTOM:

Fine, Lecoing. Now there's reasoning which does you honor, and which strikes me! Come on! I shall then go into your forest, well assured that my virtue will not succumb to any attempt.

LECOING:

On that note, to our business. And at midnight at the Duke's oak.

(All disperse)

BOTTOM:

Flute, would you, my young man, be like me, one day, the honor of your sex? Well—(he leaves last with Flute, chiding him)

CURTAIN

ACT I

Scene 3

A clearing in the Forest. The Duke's oak. Night. The moon shines.

OBERON: (with his suite, calling)

Hola! My gay goblins! Get over here, Puck! Help me.

PUCK: (appearing)

Oberon! Here I am my good master, my king, whose fool I am.

OBERON:

Sparrow whose eagle I am. What prank, tell me, are you playing, my rogue?

PUCK:

I was I don't know where, wandering to and fro. I am weary!

OBERON:

So your profession is very tiring?

PUCK:

Don't tell me about it! From dawn till dusk, you must work or play; just to have something to do. Think of it. The flowers have bejeweled me! I have their confidence and I have their customers. I must deliver them in bunches. All their precious jewels, stock their shops, with opals, sapphires, pearls, diamonds; to furnish all, from lilies to daisies;

from carnations, rubies, sewn on velour, from buttonholes, or collars, hanging with dew, to bears' ears. If my clientele pays well, I could still economize. But all get their money back, after having paid you with a kiss. Ah, the situation is hard. But there are men, who, luckily, are dummies, fatuous, and malefactors, to make us laugh a little, shabby creatures that we are, and they make truly amusing playthings! They are my puppets, all these fine wannabe saints! My master, I laugh like a god to see them; some weep, others tremble. I damn them all, that's my duty! Sparing only those who are not stupid. I will exempt only lovers and poets from all malicious pranks. Those who make love, those who make love.

OBERON:

Puck, do you have any news of Titania, for we are squabbling?

PUCK:

Why, you are coming to her place.

OBERON:

I don't want to see her and I'm avoiding her.

PUCK:

Now's the time she always emerges. Here she is.

(Enter Titania with her suite of fairies.)

OBERON:

Eh, what! Titania! Bothersome meeting!

TITANIA:

Is that Oberon that the Moon is showing me? Let's fly away from here.

OBERON:

No! I am your lord. Stay!

TITANIA:

Then treat your lady with honor.

OBERON:

And you, deal with my jealousy a little. Be less eager to go to your fantasy, towards strong-armed Theseus, your admiration!

TITANIA:

And are you going to temper your grand passion for beautiful Hippolyta with her sweet wild glances? Isn't it for her, for her wedding, that you've just rushed from the depths of the Orient? And since when, with us, is it such a crying wrong to follow, with a soul uneasy or delighted, the great human actors in the drama of life?

OBERON:

Yes, that's fair! Let's loan ourselves a compassionate heart to the sorrows, to the battles of mankind, these passers-by who sniff error around them in Nature, mysterious witnesses of the sober adventurers, the spirits, and who have in joy or boredom unknown friends always leaning over them! But I have other griefs! Wicked one, you are keeping that page from me, that child whose grace enchants me. Give him back to me, I'll give you back my heart.

TITANIA:

Triumphant king, your realm, in my eyes, isn't worth this child. His mother was my sister. In the soft breezes of the Indies, we were seated on the shore, looking on the sea. The sails waved and we laughed to see them. Under the kisses of the wind, they billowed out and conceived the unlimited, then, throwing herself to swimming when her blessed flank bore my little page; Madwoman, she pushed him before her, and skimming the waves, brought me back this small thing now, like a rich ship with a big cargo, filled with delightful booty from its bold course. But she was mortal and died of this son, and I am keeping him, despite prayers and threats, this child who revives my faithful companion and that I shall always love for love of her.

OBERON:

Is that your last word?

TITANIA:

Yes. Stay, if you wish under the gentle moonlight to contemplate our sport. If not, g'd-bye!

OBERON:

The child! Give him to me, I'll stay.

TITANIA:

No. Even if you were offering me all the celestial empire! But I'm afraid of failing in what I owe to myself, and I'm leaving you.

(She leaves with her fairies)

Go, ingrate! Before leaving this forest you shall pay me dearly for your offence. Help me, Puck, my sweet Puck, come serve my vengeance. You know the flower—it used to be white, red at present—that an arrow of Cupid dipped in wounding the Chimera of love. Two drops pressed from the chalice on the closed eyes of a man or a woman, during sleep, have this strange effect: on awakening, the sleeper before whose eyes teasing fate causes to appear, be it the worst animal, lion, bull, monkey or bear, this suddenly becomes his dream or her passion. Well, go find that flower for me.

PUCK:

In less than an hour I can circle our globe. But the magic flower, what! You'd test it on the Queen?

OBERON:

Go run, return and you shall see.

(Puck leaves running)

CURTAIN

ACT II

Scene 4

In the forest. Same set as Scene III.

OBERON: (alone, striding around impatiently)

What! To cross the great blue zones, barely two or three damned leagues, to take ten minutes already! Puck, that goblin of the breeze has become as slothful as thunder and lightning! Someone's coming. These humans, their joy and their distress touch me. To listen to them and watch them interests me. Let's listen.

(hiding himself)

DEMETRIUS: (entering pursued by Helena)

Leave me alone! Will you get away from me!

HELENA:

No! You're seeking Lysander! You intend to fight with him! Ah, wretched woman that I am! Why did I apprise you of the secret of Hermia's flight? I intended to persuade you that there was no longer any reason for you to think of her; I also wanted to entice you into thinking of me a little. But what I did for love, you are twisting to hate.

DEMETRIUS:

Yes, Hermia is killing me. I will kill Lysander! Leave me alone, I tell you!

HELENA:

And leave you to this duel, in this danger? Never!

DEMETRIUS:

Do you want me to detest you?

HELENA:

Can you imagine that is what I want?

DEMETRIUS:

You are forcing me at the very least to repeat that I do not love you, that I love Hermia, no one but Hermia for all my life.

HELENA:

You are cruel, Demetrius!

DEMETRIUS:

Hey! All you have to do is stop following me around.

HELENA:

No! Even when your words to me are so harsh, the sound of your voice is sweet to me. And besides, if you find Lysander and if you attack him, I have to be there to throw myself between you, to be struck in your place who knows? To die by your hand, perhaps? Oh, no, surely I will not stop following you.

DEMETRIUS:

Well, as for me, I won't stop insulting you.

HELENA:

As you like. I shall not hear the maledictions from your mouth. I'll listen to the blessings of my heart.

DEMETRIUS:

I hate you! I hate you!

(Demetrius leaves)

HELENA: (following him)

I love you! I love you!

OBERON: (emerging)

Poor child! I intend your sorrow to change to joy before dawn comes.

(Enter Puck with a bunch of flowers in hand)

PUCK:

I have the flower.

OBERON:

Thanks, Puck! In these woods I know a retreat that's charming, secret, and made of perfumed shadows. Thyme, blindweed, daffodils, violets, are the variegated sward; the lily, the honeysuckle of penetrating aroma, myrtle, jasmine, rose are the dome. There, my Titania closes here her gently inclining eyes. I'm flying there, and with a flower, I'll punish the rebel.

(delivering a bunch of flowers to Puck) Search the forest. You will see a beauty weeping, chasing after a young, frigid Athenian that she loves and stalks. You will dampen the eyes of the disdainful youth with the lucky flower, so he will be more in love than she is! For the philter to have this effect on him, he must see her when he wakes.

PUCK:

That's understood, it's done.

(Oberon and Puck leave; Lysander and Hermia enter.)

HERMIA:

Decidedly, Lysander, you've lost your way.

LYSANDER:

I beg you to believe it, my poor beloved. Yes, I have lost my way in the paths of this great thick forest.

HERMIA:

Because—look how long we've been walking, you know. I admit I feel a bit weary.

LYSANDER:

Well, let's stop and you rest. Luckily, June nights are short, and dawn, when it comes, will show us our path. Hold on, here's a grassy slope which seems to invite sleep.

Stretch your delicate limbs out there and I will stay beside you to protect you, and to gaze at you.

HERMIA:

Beside me! Not at all, no. If you please, good Lysander, take it for yourself, this hillock. As for me, it suffices that I know where you are. For my part, I'm going to find some other mossy bed nearby.

LYSANDER:

You want that?

HERMIA:

My dear friend, I beg you.

LYANDER:

Then, my dear wife, I have only to obey you.

HERMIA: (distancing herself)

Good night, sweet friend! Don't forget me in your dreams!

(she leaves)

LYSANDER: (stretching on the lawn)

Neither in my dreams nor in my life, or my soul, love!

(he dozes off)

PUCK: (enters, looking around)

Yes, it's she. She's going looking, pretty soul, for her miser of love. Yes, I've found the woman; but the man?

(noticing Lysander) Ah, who's snoozing there? I've got my uncivil one.

(waving the magic flower sack over his eyes) With my bud trap, my beautiful flighty bud, I've caught you.

(he leaves, laughing)

HELENA: (entering, calling)

Demetrius! Demetrius! Where are you? He's escaped me. If he's gone to meet Lysander! Suppose Lysander kills him! Ah, I'm the one he'd have killed.

(noticing Lysander) Who's stretched out there? Demetrius?

(leaning over him) No. It's Lysander. Could he be dead? Struck down by my valiant Demetrius? Lysander! Lysander, wake up, if you are alive.

LYSANDER: (waking and uttering a cry of admiration)

Ah, yes, I'm alive. And my life belongs to you forever, incomparable beauty.

HELENA:

Lysander, you are mistaken, I'm not Hermia, I'm Helen.

LYSANDER:

No, I'm not mistaken. Who could I confuse with your celestial face? Hermia! What's Hermia beside you? A crow beside a dove!

HELENA:

Are you dreaming or are you mad, Lysander?

LYSANDER:

I was dreaming and I was mad, when you, being there, I could only look at Hermia.

HELENA:

Oh! Why are you making fun of me, Lysander? Repulsed by Demetrius must I also be mocked by you? I thought you a lord of greater courtesy.

LYSANDER: (throwing himself at her feet)

Me make sport of you! Me? When I adore you!

HELENA: (getting loose)

Ah, this is too much, and I'm leaving the place to you.

(Lysander follows her)

HELENA:

Stay! I forbid you to follow me.

(she leaves)

LYANDER:

Prevent the magnet affection turning north, prevent the star from turning in its sphere.

(running after her)

(Enter Bottom, two apprentices bearing a hamper on which are the costumes. Etrigne with his lion head in his arm. The Wall is played by a man dressed and smeared white. The Moon is represented by a man carrying a bunch of twigs, holding a lantern in his hand.)

BOTTOM:

This way, gang, this way!

LECOING:

I am hoping to see a superb place for our rehearsal.

FLUTE:

The green will be our stage, and this hawthorn thicket our wings.

BOTTOM: (taking Lecoing aside)

Peter Lecoing! I've studied my role as Pyramus and I have a few minor things to say to you about that.

LECOING: (grimacing)

Ah! What's that?

BOTTOM:

In the ending, I pull my sword and kill myself. That lacks gayety. The public is never happy to be sad, you see, and when a play doesn't end happily, it ends badly.

FLUTE: (to Groin)

What a deep man!

LECOING:

So, Bottom, you think we must change the ending?

BOTTOM:

No need. Only make me a prologue, and let this Prologue be made to say that we have no intention of harming ourselves with our swords, that Pyramus isn't killing himself for real, and that in the end I am really not Pyramus but Bottom the weaver. Then, you grasp, no more emotion is possible.

LECOING:

Well, that's an idea! We will have a prologue, Bottom, a fine prologue in twelve foot verse.

BOTTOM:

Let it have fourteen or fifteen, who cares! It will only go better.

ETRINGE:

Dear Bottom, one word, I beg you. If the role of Pyramus is a bit sad, think of the role of the lion. How terrible that is!

BOTTOM:

Ah! Certainly, to lead a lion into the midst of ladies is serious! We don't have any birds of prey more terrifying than a lion, everyone knows that.

ETRIGNE:

Don't talk to me about it! Even I who will be the lion, I'll make myself tremble. Well, Bottom, won't this be in the prologue, a way to prepare the public a little, to slip in a word on the subject of the lion?

BOTTOM:

Ah, my good friend, don't take my effects from me, I beg you! My prologue belongs to me and to me alone.

ETRIGNE: (supplicating)

But then, good Bottom, what to do?

BOTTOM:

Come on, listen, Etrigne, I advise you to let your nose pass squarely under your mane of hair, and to speak to yourself and say: "My beautiful ladies, I beg you not to be frightened, they're going to hang me. If you imagine I am a living lion, I shall be a dead man." After that, tell 'em your name, and admit frankly that you are Etrigne, the tinker.

ETRIGNE:

Ah, very nice, very nice! Thanks, good Bottom, thanks.

BOTTOM:

Now, if you'd care to begin—

LECOING:

Right away. Finish putting on your costumes, sons of your mothers.

(All withdraw to the rear and dress in their costumes. Enter Puck)

PUCK: (to the side)

Who are these thick comedians coming without fear to rehearse their fat parts on the lawn where our king and our queen with white forms, awaken, gentle quarrelers, the bird songs under these branches, and the perfumes in these flowers? Oh, but we will avenge our arbors, and free our lawns, and cherished flowers of these caterpillars, our dear birds of these ninnies.

(hiding)

LECOING:

Where are we? Aren't you all quite permeated with the gentle feelings of your lamentable parts? Come on, the two lovers, the fathers, poor mothers, the lion, the moonlight. You, too, Wall. Tears in every eye.

(all gravely come forward; Lecoing sits on the grass, manuscript in hand) We say then that the first scene is between Pyramus and Thisbe. You Wall, stand up tall. You, Moonlight give light.

(Wall extends his arm and spreads his finger. The Man on the Moon waves his lantern. Pyramus and Thisbe are on each side of Wall.)

BOTTOM:

I begin. "Odorous flowers."

LECOING: (whistling)

No, Bottom, "Odiferous flowers."

BOTTOM: (impatiently)

Ah, right. Let's see. Odorous, odiferous, that's a joke, really. Do you imagine the public notices things like that? Come on, what was I saying Odious flowers.

LECOING: (whistling)

Odiferous, odiferous!

BOTTOM: (shrugging)

Pedant!

(resuming) "Odiferous flowers have a perfume less sweet, than your breath, my Thisbe." Let's take a breather after breath.

LECOING: (looking at his script)

After breath.

PUCK: (aside)

Just wait! I'm going to make you breathe, I am.

(splaying his mouth with both hands and whistling)

BOTTOM: (sneezes.)

Achoo! Come on! Right! See the evening cold. Well, as for me, you see, it always has the same effect that the stars do on me; they give me a cold.

FLUTE: (following his part)

That's not my reply.

BOTTOM:

Hold on a sec, Thisbe. I have my nightcap, that my apprentice must have put in my bag. Hey, little fellah, where are you?

PUCK: (in the shadows)

Here, boss.

(aside) I'm going to adjust your costume, so that your face will forget distracted nature.

FLUTE:

But, Lecoing, there's no nightcap in his part. He's adding to it! He's adding to it!

BOTTOM: (coming back with an ass's head)

What is it I'm adding?

(general screams of terror)

FLUTE:

Help!

BOTTOM: (shouting, too)

What? What is it? What's wrong?

FLUTE:

A monster!

BOTTOM: (terrified)

A monster! Where?

ALL:

There! You! You!

BOTTOM: (shrugging his shoulders)

Me, a monster!

LECOING:

Wretch! Feel your ears!

BOTTOM:

Help me! Is this a farce? My friends—

(Shouts, confusion, Puck pursues them and throws stones at them)

PUCK: (harassing them)

Watch your skin! Dog, flame, pincers, I gnaw, burn, and whip!

(The abused troupe all escape bewildered. The lion and Bottom remain, both in shock)

BOTTOM: (holding the lion by his tail)

Etrigne, my brave lion!

ETRIGNE: (turning and roaring)

RRRROARRR!

BOTTOM: (recoiling and braying)

WHHEYYY!

(Etrigne takes flight)

Will you look at that? Such asses!

(following them braying)

CURTAIN

ACT II

Scene 5

Another part of the forest.

TITANIA: (stretched out on a flowery thicket with fairies around her)

Sing to us now your even-song, and after that, let each do her duty. Go, my sisters, kill the worm at the rosebud, who would kill it before it blooms. Prune from the wings of bats little grey dresses for a small blue sylph. Hunt the barn owl, prepare the toilet of flowers, from the lily to the violet. And place grains of flattery in pistoles of gold. But first of all, sing us your even-song.

FIRST FAIRY: (singing)

Woodland stream, 'neath the moss
Make all pebbles silent
My queen is dozing, she is sweet.
Woodland breezes be gentle.

CHORUS OF FAIRIES:

Nightingale 'neath the arbor
Sing to my charmed queen.
Lullaby, lullaby, lullaby!
Night, on my dozing queen
Make the friendly star gaze.

(a ray of starlight rests on Titania)

Star, go to her, there she is!

SECOND FAIRY: (singing)

My queen is charming and tender
Be gone from here prowling serpents,
Spiders, blind worms, salamanders,
Evil and ugly!

FIRST FAIRY: (singing)

She's sleeping! Cradle my queen
Sweet silence, serene shadows.

(The fairies distance themselves. Titania sleeps. Oberon and Puck enter stealthily)

OBERON:

Come. I'm going to pour mysterious enchantments on her eyes.

(going to Titania and pressing the magic flower on her eyelids)

When you wake, let the first-comer be your master, and your blind love. Were he a hideous monster he must appear to you as beautiful as the dawn. Love him, stupid or vile, love him ugly or treacherous. Love and suffer in your turn.

(Bottom is heard braying in the distance) What's that commotion?

PUCK: (bursting into laughter)

Ha, ha!

OBERON:

Hush!

PUCK: (dragging him away)

Come, I've got to laugh. Chance understands mockery much better than we do!

CURTAIN

ACT III

Scene 6

Another part of the forest. A very thick and confused area, a sort of labyrinth of verdure completely entangled with hillocks, paths and underbrush. The darkness is even more profound and mysterious here.

OBERON: (entering with Puck)

What a bore! You must cure an inconstant.

PUCK: (laughing)

Now that's what I'm doing twice.

OBERON:

Still, we've got to get it over with. Night is passing. Light is not to be feared. And the game I hunt, often, in the morning, leaves its thickets at the vermilion moment when the Orient opens the gates of the Sun to its foggy horizon as the bitter, threatening sea, abruptly makes the flame run, drawn passionately through the infinite net of quivering enlargement, and changes the green salt of the water into purple gold.

(noticing Demetrius asleep) Hey, why, hold on, here's the one Helena adores, the one who disdains her and that she still adores. Here he is.

PUCK:

Great! Wait! There, in that part of the forest, I just now thought I saw Helena.

(starts to go and stops, cocking his ear) That's her voice. She's calling. Yes, here's our love in tears. Quick, let's apply the philter and its sweet charms to the sleeper.

OBERON: (dropping the juice of the flower on Demetrius's eyes.)

Love the one you see when your eyes are opened.

PUCK: (laughing)

Fine! First, no one loved her, and now both will love her!

(Oberon and Puck conceal themselves)

HELENA: (enters, calling)

Demetrius!

(turning to Lysander) Lysander, won't you give up this odious pursuit?

LYSANDER:

Command me to die, but not to leave you.

HELENA: (calling)

Demetrius!

DEMETRIUS: (waking up)

Who's calling me?

HELENA:

Demetrius! Ah! At last! Demetrius, you no longer love me as your fiancée, but at least show me respect as your relative.

DEMETRIUS: (contemplating her with delight)

Helena!

LYANDER:

Oh! Now Demetrius and I are going to understand each other. Friend, it's Hermia that you love. I am going to give up to you all my rights to Hermia. As for me, she who I love to the point of losing my reason, is ravishing Helena.

DEMETRIUS:

The divine Helena! Hey, but, me, too wretch, it's Helena that I love!

HELENA:

What! Are you joining with him to mock me, Demetrius?

LYSANDER:

Yes, it's bad, Demetrius, you love Hermia that's not a reason to make fun of Helena.

DEMETRIUS:

You are jesting, beauty-without-parallel. You jest, ideal nymph! But listen to me; look at me! Does one jest when prostrating himself? Does one mock on one's knees?

HELENA:

Maybe! You are giving me your love, Demetrius! Ah, I knew well enough that with the power of gentleness and tenderness, I would end by reconquering you.

DEMETRIUS:

It's not a question of tenderness and gentleness; I love you because I love you. I love you because my heart is breaking when I contemplate you; I love you because there's no queen in the world worthy of being your servant.

LYSANDER: (folding his arms indignantly)

Well, but Hermia? Hermia, that you loved so distractedly, ingrate!

DEMETRIUS:

Hermia! Come off it! Though my heart may have stopped a minute for her, it has now returned to Helena, as to its center, and as to its hearth, to fix itself there forever. Keep your Hermia, Lysander! I care for her as I do this withered leaf!

HERMIA: (in the distance, calling)

Lysander!

DEMETRIUS:

Hold on, there she is, your beauty.

HERMIA: (entering) Lysander!

Oh, naughty. Where are you? Why have you left me?

LYSANDER:

I left you because love called me elsewhere.

HERMIA:

Elsewhere than where I am?

LYSANDER:

Yes. Where a more radiant star attracts me than that which shines at this moment over our heads, there where I followed Helena.

DEMETRIUS: (striding to Lysander)

Lysander! Don't assume these passionate poses when speaking of my Helena! I forbid you to do it.

LYSANDER:

Ah, and will you also forbid my heart to beat?

DEMETRIUS: (pulling his sword)

I will surely prevent it with the help of this sword.

LYSANDER: (pulling his)

Unless this one finds your heart first!

HELENA: (throwing herself between them)

Demetrius! Ah, come help me, Hermia. Before they wanted to fight over you; now they want to kill themselves for me.

HERMIA: (striding to Helena and grabbing her by the arm)

Why, it's actually true! It's actually possible.

DEMETRIUS: (lowering his voice)

Lysander! Come! Let me tell you.

(they talk to each other animatedly, but we cannot hear them)

HERMIA:

Ah! Trickster! Love thief! Corroder of flowers! You come at night to steal the heart of my lover!

HELENA:

Hermia! For mercy sakes, let's think only of appeasing them.

HERMIA:

Ah, you are afraid.

HELENA:

Yes, for them.

LYSANDER: (low and quickly to Demetrius)

It's settled. Let's separate. I'll await you there at the lime tree that you see at the entrance to the clearing.

DEMETRIUS: (low to Lysander)

Don't make me wait too long.

(They leave in different directions)

HELENA: (to Hermia)

Ah, wait, they're getting away from us.

(she follows Demetrius)

HERMIA: Oh, let's not leave them.

(looking for Lysander) Lysander! Where'd he go?

(she leaves in the same direction that he went)

OBERON:

They are leaving to fight and slaughter each other, you see.

PUCK:

No. Don't worry about a thing. I'm going to counterfeit their voices and confuse their steps, using this thicket as an accomplice, to prevent such a stupid plan from coming to fruition.

(Oberon and Puck leave. Lysander and Demetrius come and go, running through the woods, one after the other. Puck appears and disappears between them.)

LYSANDER:

Well, Demetrius? Must I come to get you, braggart? Where are you? Show yourself, if a flicker of courage remains in your heart.

PUCK: (behind the trees)

Here, poltroon! Sword in hand and on guard!

LYSANDER: Here I am! Here I am!

(he leaves following Puck's voice.)

DEMETRIUS: (entering)

Lysander! You are here. Speak again. Ah, coward, ah. Runaway! Where are you hiding? In this thorny thicket? Under what pile of rocks?

PUCK: (hidden)

Hey! It's you, prudent man, shielding yourself in this thick briar patch. As for me, I'm waiting for you where the Moon is hiding. Here, where the terrain is flat.

DEMETRIUS:

Fine! I'll join you, wretch!

LYSANDER: (entering)

Didn't you say they you would meet me? Yes, but while waiting you don't budge from this black copse where you crouch like a jack-rabbit. Oh, I'll end yet by finding you and killing you in your hare's lair. Where are you?

PUCK:

Right here. I'm calling you loud enough, it seems to me.

LYSANDER:

Ah, at last.

(he rushes to the right)

DEMETRIUS: (coming back)

Scoundrel, in place of a heart you've got legs! When I get where you call me, you're already gone. But, timid mole, wherever you may be, I will unearth you.

PUCK:

I am here. Can't you hear me?

DEMETRIUS:

Stay right there for just two seconds.

(rushing out left)

LYSANDER: (entering breathless)

No one! Nothing! What cowardice!

I can't take it any more!! This course of hide and seek has put me out of breath.

(raising his voice.) Listen, cowardly Demetrius. I am going to stretch out at the very foot of the tree where I gave you a rendezvous. If you don't come to find me here before this night is over, I will find you, yes, I will, when day begins.

(leaves by the left)

PUCK: (reappearing, and calling)

Hermia! Hermia! My Hermia!

HERMIA'S VOICE: (off)

Lysander, is that you calling me?

PUCK:

Yes, over here! Come!

(pulling the magic flower) Flower of mocking love. Blind and uncertain flower. Come, reopen in this heart it's first wound.

(Puck vanishes as if following Lysander)

HERMIA: (entering) Lysander!

Where are you? Night is so dark in this copse, Lysander!

VOICE OF PUCK: (off)

Hermia.

HERMIA: (looking to the left)

Ah, I see him down there, stretched out under that lime tree. He's asleep.

(leaves) My Lysander, wake up.

PUCK: (Coming back and watching her)

Come on, will you! How much trouble one has to make between them to elude two enemies and to join to lovers!

CURTAIN

ACT III

Scene 7

Same as Scene 4. Titania's retreat.

Titania is dozing as Bottom enters.

BOTTOM:

Ah, yes, yes, I see their shame! They would like to make me pass in my own eyes for a donkey! Never! Bottom has a powerful head! Bottom's going to sing to prove he's not afraid.

(sings)

Nice cuckoo, in the willowed woods,
Cuckoo! Your call resounds.
A serious call to which
None will say no. Unless he's mad.
Cuckoo! Cuckoo!

TITANIA: (wakened by the singing and perceiving Bottom.)

Ah! What angel wakes me in my bed of flowers?

BOTTOM:

Come on, great! I'm bumping into a fairy!

TITANIA:

Charming mortal! Your voice is as sweet to my ears as your beauty ravishes my eyes. I love you.

BOTTOM:

You love me! You love me! But, 'scuse me, Madame, I don't know you.

TITANIA:

His wit is worthy of his radiant face.

BOTTOM:

My wit! I wish I had merely enough to find my way back.

(Titania places her hand on his shoulder) Look, let me go away, Madame! Leave me alone.

(He gets loose kicking)

TITANIA:

Will you or nill you, you shan't escape from my prison of roses and leaves!

BOTTOM:

Well, this is gay!

TITANIA:

Why look at me, will you! I am a divinity! My empire is one of eternal summer, and I love you! At my voice, your servants, the Fairies will come place flowers on your glorious face. They'll go to seek pearls in the depths of the seas for you. They will cradle you with their sweetest concerts. Plundered of your fleshly envelope, you will be, like myself, a breath, a dream, a soul, a wing!

BOTTOM:

Madame, I warn you, you are talking jargon! Useless for me to open wide my ears. I don't understand a thing.

TITANIA: (calling)

Help me!

(Fairies and sylphs surround her)

BOTTOM:

Ah, trouble! The whole band now!

TITANIA:

Come my little fairies. Come, all un-made-up. Serve my beloved lord. Pillage the hive, and the vine arbor, and devastate the flower bed of flowers and the fruits of May.

BOTTOM:

No, no, no flowers, no fruits! Let 'em bring me a truss of hay and a good peck of oats.

TITANIA: (placing a crown of flowers on his head)

O my king, let your queen crown you with verbena, and caress you gently with her vermillion lips, and stroke your long beautiful ears, O my ideal lover!

BOTTOM:

No, you are all tickling me, you are tickling me. Let 'em scratch me! Let 'em scratch me!

(calling fairies) Hey! You there! Young-uns! Scratch my head a little. Harder, harder! Even harder!

TITANIA:

Dance, my sisters. Charm his eyes by grouping knowingly your harmonious bodies!

(rondeaux and fairy dance)

BOTTOM:

Well, no. All these gyrations do not charm my eyes, they confuse 'em.

TITANIA: (leading him to a flower thicket)

Come! Place on my heart your dear enormous head! Come, and like the ivy on the trunk of the elm, let your humble slave, o my indulgent master, enlace you in her arms, beautiful angel with silver skin.

(Bottom falls into a deep sleep)

TITANIA: (seeing Oberon and screaming)

Ah! Are you coming to carry away my beloved from me, profane man!

OBERON: (stretching out his wand)

You see who he really is.

TITANIA:

A donkey!

OBERON:

A donkey! Yes, goddess, this is your passion.

TITANIA:

An ass! And I see him!

OBERON:

And you love him still!

TITANIA: (struggling, resisting)

Oh, why I'll break this love and your trap! No. The trap's holding me! Ah, this is sorcery! Let it up. Pity! I'm crying!

OBERON:

Give me your page.

TITANIA:

No.

OBERON:

Goodbye.

TITANIA:

Cruel! He's yours.

OBERON: (tenderly)

He's ours. Thanks!

(extending his hand)

From this face of light
Steal away, impure folly, crude shade.

114 * *The Dream of a Summer Night*, by Paul Meurice

TITANIA: (eyes opened, looking at Bottom)

Ah! What a horror! I loved this monster. Dear Mocker. Where shall I flee? Where hide my shame?

OBERON:

On my heart.

(she throws herself into his arms)

Our battle on the subject of Hippolyta and Theseus is actually appeased. Let's go to their palace before dawn to bring our gifts of joy and our wishes of love.

TITANIA: (with kindness to Puck, pointing to Bottom)

Puck. Make it so he dreamed it.

OBERON:

Come, my dear diaphanous Queen.

(They leave with their suites)

PUCK: (removing Bottom's ass's head)

Lose you ass's head and watch your ass's eyes.

(He leaves. The other players enter)

BOTTOM:

HeeHAW, HEEhaw. Thistles! Thistles! A big bunch of thistles!

VOICES: (outside)

Bottom! Bottom!

BOTTOM: (waking)

Hey! What! What's the matter?

ALL: (entering)

Ah, there you are! At last!

LECOING:

And he's got his own head! What's happened to you, really, Bottom?

BOTTOM:

Ah, gang, I had a dream!

LECOING:

Well, but day's coming and we've got just enough time to go take our place in the wedding procession.

BOTTOM:

Let's get going. And on the way, I'll tell you my dream. It seemed to me, I was— It seemed to me I had— Oh, it's the most prodigious adventure that ever made the ears of an—(coughs)—stand up. Ears—

(All leave.)

CURTAIN

ACT III

Scene 8

The outskirts of Theseus' new palace. Fairy-like architecture erected on the slope of a hillock. Terraces, arcades, large stairways, long galleries in the style of the old Renaissance; everywhere greenery and flowers, orange trees, myrtles—roses are mixed with marble and stone. It's still night. Slight glimmer of dawn.

Oberon, Titania, Puck, elves, and fairies bring palms and flowers. They spread them and run everywhere, wearing bows, shedding rose petals.

OBERON:

Palace where two radiant destinies are going to join, we are coming to sacrifice to you, palace, and to bless you, with songs in chorus, and flowers in glory, which are owed to heroes by genies and fairies.

CHORUS OF FAIRIES:

Flowers, colors, feast for eyes.
Flowers of gold, purple and silk
In the radiant place
Blaze out like glory!
In this radiant place
Flowers, perfume, incense, cinnamon
Penetrate senses and soul
Perfuming as with love.

Goblins, let the mad rondeau
Laugh and sing, twist and fly!

FIRST FAIRY:

For joy and for honor
All the elves and the graces
Impregnate the air on your spoor
With roses and joy!

TITANIA:

May the spouse be neat, thrifty, and faithful,
And always smiling in her fidelity.

OBERON:

May the spouse, gentle and strong and always
   taken with her,
Smolder over her, and calmly protect her.

(Dawn breaks. At a sign from Oberon the fairies and the elves distance themselves.)

The Dream of a Summer Night, by Paul Meurice * 121

CHORUS: (as it departs)

No envy of love.
It's its turn
It's dawn.

(Oberon, Titania, Puck, and the fairies disappear.)

Entrance of the marriage procession. Triumphal march. Theseus and Hippolyta under a dais. Helena giving her hand to Demetrius, Hermia giving her hand to Lysander. In the procession, Bottom. Lecoing, actors, etc. Athenians. amazons, etc.

At the end of the procession, in the rear, a luminous cloud, Oberon, and Titania with Puck beside them.

CURTAIN

ABOUT FRANK J. MORLOCK

FRANK J. MORLOCK has written and translated many plays since retiring from the legal profession in 1992. His translations have also appeared on Project Gutenberg, the Alexandre Dumas Père web page, Literature in the Age of Napoléon, Infinite Artistries.com, and Munsey's (formerly Blackmask). In 2006 he received an award from the North American Jules Verne Society for his translations of Verne's plays. He lives and works in México.

www.ingramcontent.com/pod-product-compliance
Lightning Source LLC
LaVergne TN
LVHW011208080426
835508LV00007B/677